YOUR KNOWLEDGE HAS VALUE

- We will publish your bachelor's and master's thesis, essays and papers

- Your own eBook and book - sold worldwide in all relevant shops

- Earn money with each sale

Upload your text at www.GRIN.com and publish for free

Bibliographic information published by the German National Library:

The German National Library lists this publication in the National Bibliography; detailed bibliographic data are available on the Internet at http://dnb.dnb.de .

Imprint:

Copyright © 2019 GRIN Verlag
Print and binding: Books on Demand GmbH, Norderstedt Germany
ISBN: 9783668980440

This book at GRIN:

https://www.grin.com/document/491407

Gabriel Kabanda

On the Theoretical Foundations of Computer Science.
An Introductory Essay

GRIN Verlag

GRIN - Your knowledge has value

Since its foundation in 1998, GRIN has specialized in publishing academic texts by students, college teachers and other academics as e-book and printed book. The website www.grin.com is an ideal platform for presenting term papers, final papers, scientific essays, dissertations and specialist books.

Visit us on the internet:

http://www.grin.com/

http://www.facebook.com/grincom

http://www.twitter.com/grin_com

ESSAY ON THEORETICAL FOUNDATIONS OF COMPUTER SCIENCE

Gabriel Kabanda

Atlantic International University

ABSTRACT

The paper presented an analytical exposition, critical context and integrative conclusion on the discussion on the meaning, significance and potential applications of theoretical foundations of computer science with respect to Algorithms Design and Analysis; Complexity Theory; Turing Machines; Finite Automata; Cryptography; and Machine Learning. An algorithm is any well-defined computational procedure that takes some value or sets of values as input and produces some values or sets of values as output. A Turing machine consists of a finite program, called the finite control, capable of manipulating a linear list of cells, called the tape, using one access pointer, called the head. Cellular automata is an array of finite state machines (inter-related). A universal Turing machine U is a Turing machine that can imitate the behavior of any other Turing machine T. Automata are a particularly simple, but useful, model of computation which were were initially proposed as a simple model for the behavior of neurons. A model of computation is a mathematical abstraction of computers which is used by computer scientists to perform a rigorous study of computation. An automaton with a finite number of states is called a Finite Automaton (FA) or Finite State Machine (FSM). The Church-Turing Thesis states that the Turing machine is equivalent in computational ability to any general mathematical device for computation, including digital computers. The important themes in Theoretical Computer Science (TCS) are *efficiency, impossibility results, approximation, central role of randomness, and reductions* (NP-completeness and other intractability results).

Table of content

Introduction

The paper presents an analytical exposition, critical context and integrative conclusion on the discussion on the meaning, significance and potential applications of theoretical foundations of computer science with respect to Algorithms Design and Analysis; Complexity Theory; Turing Machines; Finite Automata; Cryptography; and Machine Learning. Theoretical Computer Science (TCS)is a subset of general computer science and mathematics that focuses on more mathematical topics of computing and includes the theory of computation (https://en.wikipedia.org/wiki/Theoretical_computer_science). An *"algorithm"* can be defined as a written process that achieves a certain goal when executed. Algorithms play an increasingly important role in selecting what information is considered most relevant to us, and search engines help us navigate massive databases of information, or the entire web (Gillispie, T., 2014, p.167). Automata (singular : automation) are a particularly simple, but useful, model of computation which were were initially proposed as a simple model for the behavior of neurons (Rao, D.C., 2016, p.16). A model of computation is a mathematical abstraction of computers which is used by computer scientists to perform a rigorous study of computation. There are several models in use, but the most commonly examined is the Turing machine.

Due to the advances in technology, computer science as a field is changing because of convergence of communications and ICT, growing massive data volumes, and growing networks and sensors. There is a great need to develop theory for the new directions.The topical areas dominating the growth of ICT and development of the theory of computer science include the following emerging technologies:

➢ *The Internet of Things (IoT)* is a system of interrelated computing devices, mechanical and digital machines, objects, animals or people that are provided with unique identifiers and the ability to transfer data over a network without requiring human-to-human or human-to-computer interaction. The Internet of things (IoT) describes the digital connection of everyday objects to the Internet in order to achieve total control over such objects.

➢ *Big Data*: "Big data are high volume, high velocity, and high variety information assets that require new forms of processing to enable enhanced decision making, insight discovery and process optimization" (https://www.gartner.com, 2012).

➢ *Data mining* (knowledge discovery in databases): Extraction of interesting (non-trivial, implicit, previously unknown and potentially useful) information or patterns from data in large databases

➢ *Convergence*: The technological convergence could be understood as a process by which the telecommunications, broadcasting and information technologies merge, including the merge of fixed, mobile, terrestrial and satellite communications and including the merge of location systems and systems of establishment of places and liaisons – technology convergence of devices, services, and networks.

➢ *Eduroam (Educational Roaming)* is a global wireless network access service for research and education. An eligible organization (research organization or education-related organization) can provide users (students, researchers, staff and faculty) with wireless access at participating institutions through the use of their home institution credentials.

Theoretical Computer Science (TCS)looks at the abstract mathematical concepts involved in computing and is the genesis of computation (https://www.sciencedirect.com/journal/theoretical-computer-science). Some of the subjects that compose TCS framework include Distributed computation, Algortihms, Cryptography, Algebra, Computational Number Theory, Data Structures, Quantum Computation, Machine Learning, and Complexity Theory. The **theory of computation** is the branch of theoretical computer science that deals with whether and how efficiently problems can be solved on a model of computation, using an algorithm. According to Rao, D.C, *et al* (2016, p.5), the theory of computation is divided into three major branches: automata theory, computability theory and computational complexity theory.

In theoretical computer science, **automata theory** is the study of abstract machines and the computational problems that can be solved using these machines. These abstract machines are called **automata** (Rao, D.C, *et al*, 2016, p.).5 This automaton consists of

- **states** (represented by circles),
- and **transitions** (represented by arrows).

As the automaton sees a symbol of input, it makes a *transition* (or *jump*) to another state, according to its **transition function** (which takes the current state and the recent symbol as its inputs). This is shown on Figure 1 below.

Figure 1: A finite automaton modelling recognition of *then* (Source: Rao, D.C., *et al*, 2016)

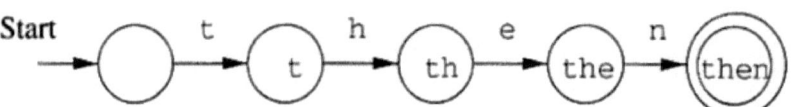

The following is a discussion on the meaning, significance and potential applications of the following theoretical foundations of computer science:

4

A. Algorithms Design and Analysis

An algorithm is any well-defined computational procedure that takes some value or sets of values as input and produces some values or sets of values as output (Cormen, T.H., *et al*, 2009). It is like a roadmap for accomplishing a task which may be simple or complex in nature. If similar tasks can be performed in a similar way, these finite steps can be converted into an algorithm making it easy for people to solve problems. The step by step procedures are written at the design stage, in any language, by someone with domain knowledge unlike the program itself which requires the expertise of a programmer to formulate the programming language. Cormen, T.H., *et al* (2009) go on to explain that an algorithm is not dependant on hardware or a software operating system.

Algorithm design is mostly concerned with creating an efficient algorithm using the least time and space. Approaches can be efficient with regards to time or be more memory efficient but these two cannot be optimised simultaneously (http://tutorials.com). The main characteristics of algorithms are that they possess a unique name, well defined set of inputs and outputs, well ordered and unambiguous operations and stop within a finite time (http://tutorials.com). Analysis of an algorithm is the determination of the amount of time and space resources required to execute it. It is important to analyse in order to determine the best algorithm for a particular problem among a number of choices. Generally the types of analyses carried out are worst case scenario, best case and average case scenarios.

Significance of Algorithms

Algorithms make it easy for people to solve problems. They can be used to automate effort for routine tasks because once an algorithm is defined, it is reusable. They can be used in large classes of problems and can be applied in domains such as science, mathematics and computers. As tools that provide well defined and efficient computational procedures, they are the core of most technologies seen in modern electronic devices. Gillespie, T. (2014) explains that algorithms help select things important to us as we navigate through the massive databases of information on various search engines and the entire web. He points out that algorithms can be considered as trusted information tools that aid public discourse. There are algorithms which help in compressing data, in sorting out millions of numbers in applying filters to images and even converting human voices to text. They give predictable results and generic solutions to problems because given valid input, they produce valid results.

5

Application of Algorithms

Frequently, we make use of algorithms without being aware of it. When we decide to go on a journey and mentally calculate the steps involved before finally choosing the best route, we are using algorithms. In computer programming, algorithms are used to help design software like in MS Office, Google, etc. Search algorithms are used to locate and retrieve specific data among a collection of data. Sort algorithms are used to save contacts on our smart phones and for Customer Lists etc in business. There are crypto-algorithms that secure access to private accounts like gmail, bank accounts etc. Algorithms also applied in performing complex addition or multiplication, division, addition or subtraction tasks. Algorithms can be used to predict random behaviour e.g in Statics and Probability, or when we use google instructions e.g how to operate certain gadgets. Future of Algorithms:- Artificial intelligence, Big Data, Machine Learning, Robotics, etc.

Gillispie, T. (2014) highlighted six dimensions of public relevance algorithms that

have political valence:

1. *Patterns of inclusion:* the choices behind what makes it into an index in the first place, what is excluded, and how data is made algorithm ready.

2. *Cycles of anticipation:* the implications of algorithm providers' attempts to thoroughly know and predict their users, and how the conclusions they draw can matter.

3. *The evaluation of relevance:* the criteria by which algorithms determine what is relevant, how those criteria are obscured from us, and how they enact political choices about appropriate and legitimate knowledge.

4. *The promise of algorithmic objectivity:* the way the technical character of the algorithm is positioned as an assurance of impartiality, and how that claim is maintained in the face of controversy.

5. *Entanglement with practice:* how users reshape their practices to suit the algorithms they depend on, and how they can turn algorithms into terrains for political contest, sometimes even to interrogate the politics of the algorithm itself.

6. *The production of calculated publics:* how the algorithmic presentation of publics back to themselves shape a public's sense of itself, and who is best positioned to benefit from that knowledge.

B. Complexity Theory

Complexity theory is concerned with the study of the intrinsic complexity of computational tasks and to understand the relations between the various phenomena in the computation (Goldreich, O., 2000). A problem is considered to be complex in proportion to the difficulty of carrying out the most efficient algorithm by which it may be decided (Walter, D., 2016). The very word complex implies diversity, large numbers and varieties of interdependent yet autonomous parts (Park, 2017). According to Cunningham, R. (2003), the key elements in systems that lend themselves to complexity analysis are that systems are dynamic, that is continuously changing and are far from equilibrium. For example, there are open systems where there is interchange of information with the surroundings and there systems where the whole is more than the sum of its parts. Cunningham, R. (2003), posits that in such systems, patterns may emerge which cannot be predicted by looking at parts of the system. Complex adaptation is where a diversion of agents interact and mutually affect each other leading to a new emergent behaviour for the whole system.

Complex, self-organising, adaptive systems possess a kind of dynamism that makes them qualitatively different from static objects such as computer chips. Complex systems are more spontaneous, more disorderly, more alive than that. Chaos theory is the qualitative study of unstable, aperiodic behaviour in deterministic, non-linear, dynamical systems (Kabanda, G., 2013). It is a specialised application of dynamical systems theory. Chaotic systems require impossible accuracy for useful prediction tasks. Chaos theory often seeks to understand the behaviour of a complex system by reconstructing its attractor, and knowing this attractor gives us qualitative understanding. Chaos theory includes theoretical hypotheses that assert relationships of qualitative (or topological) similarity between its abstract models and the actual systems it studies. Dynamics is used more as a source of qualitative insight than for making quantitative predictions. Its great value is its adaptability for constructing models of natural systems, which models can then be varied and analysed comparatively easily (Kabanda, G., 2013). Chaos theory is the quantitative study of dynamic non-linear system. Non-linear systems change with time and can demonstrate complex relationships between inputs and outputs due to reiterative feedback loops within the system. These systems are predictable but their behaviour is exquisitely sensitive to their starting point. Chaos is a sub-discipline of complexity. Complexity theory is the qualitative aspect drawing upon insights and metaphors that are derived from chaos theory.

There are three aspects of Chaos that relate to fractal patterns, bounded infinity, and unpredictability (Smitherman, S., 2014, p.6):

1. Fractal Patterns

   Fractals are patterns of self-similarity that are generated using iterated functions. The word fractal is a way to describe geometric patterns that do not become more simplified (reduced) as one zooms in or out. According to Smitherman (2014, p.6), patterns of behavior in a classroom can relate to these fractal patterns. Still others are chaotic, like the behavior of students that are performed each day in the classroom. These fractaled patterns display dynamic relations that occur within a classroom among teachers, students, subject material and the classroom environment. By relating conversations in the classroom to fractal patterns, teachers can embrace

7

a rich metaphor as a picture of what is occurring. The initial seed will have an impact on what conversation will ensue, the format of the discussion will affect the type of interaction, and the patterns of the resulting conversation may in fact display differing "orbits."

2. Bounded Infinity

Consider all the numbers that exist on a number line between the integers of zero and one. That is one example of a bounded set of an infinite amount of members. Teachers can connect to this notion of bounded infinity in their classrooms. A teacher may be restricted (bounded) by the national initiatives, state mandates, district criteria, school instructions, and curricular concerns, but within these boundaries are infinite possibilities. The potential relationships between teacher and students, among students, and how a teacher chooses to implement the subject material are boundless. This grants freedom to the teacher to not feel constricted by the limits that are imposed by outside sources but rather to be creative within them (Smitherman, S., 2014, p.9).

3. Unpredictability

Chaos theory incorporates the notion that sensitive dependence to initial conditions is an important component needed to generate chaotic behaviors. Small variations in conditions may lead to large differences in nonlinear dynamical systems. Non-linear, open systems are divergent and generative, not closed and limited. An immediate consequence of sensitive dependence in any system is the impossibility of making perfect predictions, or even mediocre predictions sufficiently far into the future. Predicting becomes problematic beyond certain ranges of time (Smitherman, S., 2014, p.10).

Significance and Application of Complexity Theory

Complexity Theory is central to computing. It helps computer scientists to relate and group problems together in complexity classes. Sometimes when a problem is solved, it may open up possibilities of solving other problems. This helps to determine complexity of a problem which is often measured by the amount of time and space it takes to solve a problem. It also helps in decision problems which can be simulated on computational models such as Turing Machines. Turing Machines are the usual models for testing a problem's complexity or where it lies on the complexity hierarchy, thus helping in algorithm design and analysis. Biologists studying neurons, Engineers in designing hardware, and Physicists building quantum computers, all apply Complexity Theory. Complexity Theory helps computer scientists to determine the limits of what a computer can and cannot do.

One of the central themes in complexity theory is the difference between determinism and nondeterminism, and the tradeoff between time and space. Complexity does not mean the same as complicated. A complicated system can be broken into parts, like an airplane. In complex systems, there are no parts, only patterns, that we recognize in that moment. The patterns mean something in relation to the entire whole, and the patterns inform what that whole might be (Ruelle, D., 1991). Systems thinking emerged in science in the 1930s where scientists looked to relationships and properties of systems, recognizing that a systems approach becomes necessary. In the next decade a group of scholars from different fields interested in the "mind" entered into a series of conversations (Smitherman, S., 2014, p.15).

C. Turing Machines

Vitanyi, P.M.B., (2012) describes the Turing Machine as a hypothetical machine proposed by Allan M Turing (1936) whose computations are intended to give an operational and formal definition of the initiative notion of computability in the discrete domain. In simple terms, Turing machine is a digital device, sufficiently easy to conform to theoretical analysis and powerful enough to embrace everything in the decree domain that is intuitively computable. As Turing claimed, any process that can be naturally called an effective procedure is realized by a Turing machine. This is known as Turing's thesis. The Church-Turing thesis states that a function on the positive integers is effectively calculable if and only if it is computable. Turing machines are machines simulating other machines, Universal Turing Machine. The Church-Turing Thesis states that the Turing machine is equivalent in computational ability to any general mathematical device for computation, including digital computers.

A Turing machine is not a machine in the ordinary sense but rather an idealized mathematical model that reduces the logical structure of any computing device to its essentials. As envisaged by Turing, the machine performs its functions in a sequence of discrete steps and assumes only one of a finite list of internal states at any given moment. The machine itself consists of an infinitely extensible tape, a tape head that is capable of performing various operations on the tape, and a modifiable control mechanism in the head that can store directions from a finite set of instructions. The tape is divided into squares, each of which is either blank or has printed on it one of a finite number of symbols. The tape head has the ability to move to, read, write, and erase any single square and can also change to another internal state at any moment. Any such act is determined by the internal state of the machine and the condition of the scanned square at a given moment. The output of the machine, i.e., the solution to a mathematical query, can be read from the system once the machine has stopped. (However, in the case of Gödel's un-decidable propositions, the machine would never stop, and this became known as the "halting problem.")

According to Vitanyi, P.M.B. (2012, p.2), a Turing machine consists of a finite program, called the finite control, capable of manipulating a linear list of cells, called the tape, using one access pointer, called the head. We refer to the two directions on the tape as right and left. The finite control can be in any one of a finite set of states Q, and each tape cell can contain a 0, a 1, or a blank B. Time is discrete and the time instants are ordered 0, 1, 2, . . . , with 0 the time at which the machine starts its computation. At any time, the head is positioned over a particular cell, which it is said to scan. At time 0 the head is situated on a distinguished cell on the tape called the start cell, and the finite control is in a distinguished state q_0. At time 0 all cells contain B_s, except for a contiguous finite sequence of cells, extending from the start cell to the right, which contain 0's and 1's. This binary sequence is called the input. The device can perform the following basic operations (Vitanyi, P.M.B., 2012, p.2):

1. It can write an element from A = {0, 1, B} in the cell it scans; and
2. it can shift the head one cell left or right.

Significance of Turing machines

By incorporating all the essential features of information processing, the Turing machine became the basis for all subsequent digital computers, which share the machine's basic scheme of an input/output device (tape and reader), memory (control mechanism's storage), and central processing unit (control mechanism). In the last three-quarter of a century the Turing machine model has proven to be of priceless value for the development of the science of data processing. All theory development reaches back to this format. The model has become so dominant that new other models that are not polynomial-time reducible to Turing machines are viewed as not realistic (the so-called polynomial-time Computability thesis).

A universal Turing machine U is a Turing machine that can imitate the behavior of any other Turing machine T (Vitanyi, P.M.B., 2012, p.5). It is a fundamental result that such machines exist and can be constructed effectively with only a suitable description of T 's finite program and input being entered on U's tape initially. To execute the consecutive actions that T would perform on its own tape, U uses T 's description to simulate T 's actions on a representation of T 's tape contents. Sucha machine U is also called computation universal (Vitanyi, P.M.B., 2012, p.5).

Application of Turing machines

- **Check Decidability.** If Turing machines cannot solve a problem in countable time then there could not be any algorithm which could solve that problem (That is the problem is un-decidable). For a decision problem if its TM halt in countable time for all finite length inputs then we can say that the problem could be solved by an algorithm in countable time.
- **Classify Problem-** Turing machines helps to classify decidable problems into classes of Polynomial Hierarchy. Suppose we found that the problem is decidable, then our target becomes how efficiently we can solve it. The efficiency can been calculated in number of steps, extra space used, length of the code/size of the FSM.
- **Design and Implement Algorithm for Practical Machines:** TM helps to propagate the idea of algorithms in other practical machines. After the successful check of the criteria we can use our practical devices/computers to design and implement algorithm.

D. Finite Automata

Automata Theory is a branch of computer science that deals with designing abstract self-propelled computing devices that follow a predetermined sequence of operations automatically. An automaton with a finite number of states is called a Finite Automaton (http://www.tutorialspoint.com). An automaton (Automata in plural) is an abstract self-propelled computing device which follows a predetermined sequence of operations automatically. An automaton with a finite number of states is called a Finite Automaton (FA) or Finite State Machine (FSM). A *finite automaton (FA)* is a device that recognizes a language (set of strings). A finite automaton (or finite state machine) is a member of a class of abstract machines whose behavior may always be described in terms of a series of states occurring at successive units of discrete time. These machines are called finite because the set of possible states is finite. The machine is in one of these states at each time step and moves to a next (but not necessarily different) state at the next time step, a process known as a state transition. Time is counted in integral units beginning at $t = 0$. A system containing only a finite number of states and transitions among them is called a finite-state transition system. Finite-state transition systems can be modeled abstractly by a mathematical model called finite automation (Rao, D.C., *et al* 2016, p.16). A finite automaton has a finite set of states with which it accepts or rejects strings. It has finite memory and an input tape; each input symbol that is read causes the machine to update its state based on its current state and the symbol read. The machine accepts the input if it is in an accept state at the end of the string; otherwise, the input is rejected.

An automaton can be represented by a 5-tuple $(Q, \Sigma, \delta, q0, F)$ (http://www.tutorialspoint.com), where:

➤ ☐ Q is a finite set of states.

➤ ☐ Σ is a finite set of symbols, called the alphabet of the automaton.

➤ ☐ δ is the transition function.

➤ ☐ q0 is the initial state from where any input is processed ($q0 \in Q$).

➤ ☐ F is a set of final state/states of Q ($F \subseteq Q$).

Finite Automaton can be classified into two types:

➤ ☐ Deterministic Finite Automaton (DFA)

➤ ☐ Non-deterministic Finite Automaton (NDFA / NFA)

Deterministic Finite Automaton (DFA) is one where, for each input symbol, one can determine the state to which the machine will move. Hence, it is called Deterministic Automaton. As it has a finite number of states, the machine is called Deterministic Finite Machine or Deterministic Finite Automaton (http://www.tutorialspoint.com).

In NDFA, for a particular input symbol, the machine can move to any combination of the states in the machine. In other words, the exact state to which the machine moves cannot be determined. Hence, it is called Non-deterministic Automaton. As it has finite number of states, the machine is called Non-deterministic Finite Machine or Non-deterministic Finite Automaton (http://www.tutorialspoint.com). An NDFA can be represented by a 5-tuple $(Q, \Sigma, \delta, q0, F)$ where:

➢ Q is a finite set of states.

➢ Σ is a finite set of symbols called the alphabets.

➢ δ is the transition function where $\delta: Q \times \Sigma \rightarrow 2^Q$ (Here the power set of Q (2Q) has been taken because in case of NDFA, from a state, transition can occur to any combination of Q states)

➢ ☐ q0 is the initial state from where any input is processed $(q0 \in Q)$.

➢ ☐ F is a set of final state/states of Q $(F \subseteq Q)$.

Significance and Application of Finite Automata

Each model in automata theory plays important roles in several applied areas. Finite automata are used in text processing, compilers, and hardware design. Context-free grammar (CFGs) is used in programming languages and artificial intelligence. Originally, CFGs were used in the study of the human languages. The significance of Infinite automata is that it forms the basis of computation. Without this theory, compilers could not do they work on the front end.

Cellular automata is an array of finite state machines (inter-related) which is characterised by the following:

➢ Lattice of sites, each lattice can take one of k values

➢ Levels of lattices implement different scales of the system

➢ Discrete in time, each site updates asynchronously depending on neighbors

➢ Every site updates according to a local pre-defined rule

➢ Fixed point and limiting cycles become common

Cellular automata are used in the field of biology, the most common example being John Conway's Game of Life. Some other examples which could be explained using automata theory in biology include mollusk and pine cones growth and pigmentation patterns. Going further, a theory suggesting that the whole universe is computed by some sort of a discrete automaton is advocated by some scientists. The idea originated in the work of Konrad Zuse,, and was popularized in America by Edward Fredkin. Automata also appear in the theory of finite fields: the set of irreducible polynomials which can be written as composition of degree two polynomials is in fact a regular language.

An automaton that computes a Boolean function is called an *acceptor*. All the states of an acceptor is either accepting or rejecting the inputs given to it. A *classifier* has more than two final states and it gives a single output when it terminates. An automaton that produces outputs based on current input and/or previous state is called a *transducer*.

The following table, Table 1, lists the differences between DFA and NDFA.

Table 1: DFA vs NDFA (Source: (http://www.tutorialspoint.com, p.5)

DFA	NDFA
The transition from a state is to a single particular next state for each input symbol. Hence it is called *deterministic*.	The transition from a state can be to multiple next states for each input symbol. Hence it is called *non-deterministic*.
Empty string transitions are not seen in DFA.	NDFA permits empty string transitions.
Backtracking is allowed in DFA	In NDFA, backtracking is not always possible.
Requires more space.	Requires less space.
A string is accepted by a DFA, if it transits to a final state.	A string is accepted by a NDFA, if at least one of all possible transitions ends in a final state.

Finite-state machines, also called finite-state automata (singular: automaton) or just finite automata are much more restrictive in their capabilities than Turing machines. Finite-state machines provide a simple computational model with many applications. We may recall the definition of a Turing machine as a finite-state controller with a movable read/write head on an unbounded storage tape. If we restrict the head to move in only one direction, we have the general case of a finite-state machine. The sequence of symbols being read can be thought to constitute the input, while the sequence of symbols being written could be thought to constitute the output. We can also derive output by looking at the internal state of the controller after the input has been read.

Its important to take note of the following observations:

➢ An alphabet is specified by giving a finite set, Σ, whose elements are called symbols.

➢ A string of length n (≥ 0) over an alphabet Σ is just an ordered n-tuple of elements of Σ, written without punctuation.

➢ A language is regular iff it is the set of strings accepted by some deterministic finite automaton.

➢ We have seen that regular languages can be specified in terms of finite automata that accept or reject strings, and equivalently, in terms of patterns, or regular expressions, which strings are to match.

13

E. Cryptography

Data is valuable and needs to be protected. The protection is from unauthorised personal within an organisation for segregation of information purposes, or from external parties with malicious intentions. Therefore, electronic data must be kept and transmitted in protected formats that restrict access only to the intended users, often called encryption or cryptography. This method of protecting data is defined as follows:

> *'The art of protecting information by transforming it (encrypting it) into an unreadable format, called cipher text. Only those who possess a secret key can decipher (or decrypt) the message into plain text. ... Cryptography is used to protect e-mail messages, credit card information, and corporate data.'* Vangie Beal (*https://www.webopedia.com/TERM/C/cryptography.html*)

Cryptographic algorithms can be classified in various ways, but the major focus is on the number of keys that are employed for encryption and decryption, and by their use. The three types of algorithms that are commonly used are (Kessler, 2019, https://www.garykessler.net/library/crypto.html)

- *Secret Key Cryptography (SKC):* Uses a single key for both encryption and decryption; also called **symmetric encryption**. Primarily used for privacy and confidentiality.

- *Public Key Cryptography (PKC):* Uses one key for encryption and another for decryption; also called **asymmetric encryption**. Primarily used for authentication, non-repudiation, and key exchange.

- *Hash Functions:* Uses a mathematical transformation to irreversibly "encrypt" information, providing a digital fingerprint. Primarily used for message integrity.'

Significance of Cryptography

The importance of cryptography in computer technology is centered on three areas, which are Authentication, Integrity and Confidentiality.

a) **Authentication** refers to correctly identifying a user of a system before they are granted access, Authentication is the process by which a user establishes his identity to a system or application (https://hitachi-id.com/resource/iam-concepts/authentication.html). Hitachi categorises authentication into three forms (https://hitachi-id.com/resource/iam-concepts/authentication.html):

   ❖ *Something the user knows, i.e., a secret, such as a password, PIN or the answer to a security question.*

   ❖ *Something the user has, such as a one-time password token, smart card or mobile phone.*

   ❖ *Something the user is, meaning a biometric measurement of the user -- his voice print, finger print, vein pattern scan, iris or retina scan or some behaviour, such as his typing cadence*

b) **Integrity,** in the context of computer systems, refers to methods of ensuring that data is real, accurate and safeguarded from unauthorized user modification (https://www.techopedia.com/definition/10284/integrity). This gives users confidence that they are dealing with authentic system developers or owners.

c) **Confidentiality** means that 'you can keep your information secret especially when you send sensitive data over a network.' (https://www.eukhost.com/blog/webhosting/importance-of-cryptography-in-degital-world/). Cryptography answers the question, how can you be sure that nobody finds out about your online transactions, personal data, or any other secret information? Failure for a platform to maintain confidentiality is a breach of trust among other breaches, which will result in a loss of users.

Applications of Cryptography

Cryptography is applied in many areas of computer technology, especially wherever information needs to be kept confidential. Even before modern computers were invented, people have always had the need to create coded messages that are only understood by the sender and the user, or the keeper of information. Particularly during wars, soldiers needed to pass information in formats that the enemy could not interpret. Captured prisoners would also send letters to their fellow soldiers or family members, written in a way that contained secret messages.

Modern cryptography is used by governments, military, financial institutions, medical institutions, space agencies, portable smart devices, social media platforms and several other sectors of business and society. The latest common use of cryptography is the creation of virtual money, called crypto-currency. *Crypto-currency* is not governed by the normal banking systems of the world. It is traded by anyone, unfortunately that also includes money launderers, terrorist financiers because normal systems cannot trace the funds' movements. The levels of encryption are very high to keep this money secure on the various platforms. The types of crypto-currency that exist so far are Bitcoin, EOS, Cardano (ADA), NEO, Monero (XMR), DASH, Zcash (ZEC), Ripple (XRP), Ether and Litecoin (LTC) as list by (Bajpai, 2019, https://www.investopedia.com/tech/most-important-cryptocurrencies-other-than-bitcoin/).

Other applications for cryptography are:

A. Protecting stored files, e.g. 'in the Encrypting File System that is integrated into Microsoft Windows, the user's private key is decrypted by the operating system when the user logs in.' (https://www.nap.edu/read/25010/chapter/4#20)

B. Full disk encryption which is additional protection to the operating system and not just the stored files, 'Additional protective measures combining operating system software and computer hardware protect the system files from modification' (https://www.nap.edu/read/25010/chapter/4#21)

C. Device locking encryption that is built to activate each time the device is locked, say a phone when the screen is locked. It can only be unlocked by the user's key entered via some code or biometrics. 'The key needed to unlock the phone is a combination of the user's passcode and the phone's hardware key (https://www.nap.edu/read/25010/chapter/4#22).

D. Virtual private networks (VPN) are a way of creating an encrypted connection between a remote user and a site (https://www.nap.edu/read/25010/chapter/4#22). This enables employees of an organisation to remain accessible on their private network regardless of their location on the globe, whilst maintaining confidentiality of their communication.

E. Secure web browsing is required particularly when users visit sites that facilitate financial transactions or communication that must be confidential. The sites, browsers and servers are encrypted to ensure data security and privacy, 'Each time a user visits an e-commerce website or a Web-based email server such as Gmail or Hotmail, he or she does so through an encrypted connection' (https://www.nap.edu/read/25010/chapter/4#23).

F. Secure messaging is a requirement for most social media platforms, such as Skype, WhatsApp, GoogleTalk and Facebook Messenger. End-to-end encryption provides the security and confidentiality of these messaging services, 'Secure messaging applications use end-to-end encryption protocols to prevent third parties as well as the messaging service provider from having access to the plaintext of messages.' (https://www.nap.edu/read/25010/chapter/4#24).

G. Protecting Confidentiality in Cloud or Third-Party Computing. 'Cloud computing and storage are changing how organizations use and manage their data and, of particular relevance here, the data of their customers.'(https://www.nap.edu/read/25010/chapter/4#25). The processing and storage of data through a third-party requires strong authentication, high system integrity and maintenance of confidentiality to instil confidence in individual and corporate users.

F. Machine Learning

Computers have always operated on commands with a set of known responses programmed into them, with no room for deviation. Technology has developed to allow computers to learn new responses based on data they receive. This helps them complete tasks that were not originally programmed into them as they interact with their users. This technology is called *Machine learning* and forms part of artificial intelligence (AI). 'Machine learning focuses on the development of computer programs that can access data and use it learn to for themselves.' (https://www.expertsystem.com/machine-learning-definition/). Machine learning requires large amounts of data to analyse for computers to learn properly. It takes time resources to achieve effective machine learning that will deliver faster, more accurate results that can identify behaviour, opportunities or risks. Thomas H. Davenport, Analytics thought leader said, 'Humans can typically create one or two good models a week; machine learning can create thousands of models a week.' (https://www.sas.com/en_us/insights/analytics/machine-learning.html).

Significance of Machine Learning

Advances in the area of machine learning provide opportunities to researchers to detect network intrusion without using a signature database. Organisations and individual users aim to improve how they work and experience life. Having computer systems that can take over some tasks that cannot be programmed in faster and more accurate ways than a human being, helps to achieve these desired improvements.

> *Things like growing volumes and varieties of available data, computational processing that is cheaper and more powerful, and affordable data storage. All of these things mean it's possible to quickly and automatically produce models that can analyze bigger, more complex data and deliver faster, more accurate results – even on a very large scale. And by building precise models, an organization has a better chance of identifying profitable opportunities – or avoiding unknown risks.*

> (Statistical Analysis System, https://www.sas.com/en_us/insights/analytics/machine-learning.html).

The benefits of using AI and machine learning in cybersecurity are as follows:

- Automated protection
- Faster response and protection
- Personalization
- Learn to adapt to the situation unobtrusively
- Usability

The major applications of Machine Learning are listed below.

Applications of Machine Learning

1. **Virtual Personal Assistants** – Computing smart devices are equipped with voice recognition applications that respond to commands given by the user. In the beginning the responses are basic and at times have errors. However, over time as the application develops the user's patterns and preferences, the responses become more complex and accurate. 'Machine learning is an important part of these personal assistants as they collect and refine the information on the basis of your previous involvement with them. Later, this set of data is utilized to render results that are tailored to your preferences.' (https://medium.com/app-affairs/9-applications-of-machine-learning-from-day-to-day-life-112a47a429d0.). Examples of such applications are Siri, Alexa, Google, etc., the more popular virtual personal assistants that can be asked to recommend a good restaurant in an area the user is visiting.

2. **Predictions while Commuting** - Traffic Predictions and Online Transportation Networks assist commuters to travel faster in the most cost effective way possible. Utilising GPS navigation services, motorists can be advised by a machine learning computer of the least congested or shortest to a predetermined destination. Users seeking public transport, can book a taxi using an application of their device. This application will search for the closest available taxi and provide an estimated cost of the journey to the desired destination, '…Jeff Schneider, the engineering lead at Uber ATC reveals in an interview that they use machine learning to define price surge hours by predicting the rider demand.' (https://medium.com/app-affairs/9-applications-of-machine-learning-from-day-to-day-life-112a47a429d0).

3. **Videos Surveillance** – Artificial intelligence learns to understand and predict human behaviour through body movement. This assists users to prevent possible mishaps in public areas. 'They track unusual behaviour of people like standing motionless for a long time, stumbling, or napping on benches etc. The system can thus give an alert to human attendants, which can ultimately help to avoid mishaps.' (https://medium.com/app-affairs/9-applications-of-machine-learning-from-day-to-day-life-112a47a429d0).

4. **Social Media Services** – 'From personalizing your news feed to better advertisements targeting, social media platforms are utilizing machine learning for their own and user benefits.' (https://medium.com/app-affairs/9-applications-of-machine-learning-from-day-to-day-life-112a47a429d0). Machine learning helps users to connect online with People they may know by learning profiles on platforms such as Facebook. Facial recognition can also help identify your connection from pictures uploaded online.

5. **Email Spam and Malware Filtering** – Through learning a user's email patterns and common recipients, machine learning can filter possible spam. Also, by learning certain code, it can detect different malware. 'the system security programs that are powered by machine learning understand the coding pattern. Therefore, they detect new malware with 2–10% variation easily and offer protection against them.' (https://medium.com/app-affairs/9-applications-of-machine-learning-from-day-to-day-life-112a47a429d0)

6. **Customer Support Services** – To reduce the dependence on large number of call centre support agents, organisations are utilising chatbots that respond to basic customer queries. With time they are learning to respond to more complex questions as they continuously interact with the clients, 'These chatbots tend to extract information from the website and present it to the customers. Meanwhile, the chatbots advances with time. They tend to understand the user

queries better and serve them with better answers' (https://medium.com/app-affairs/9-applications-of-machine-learning-from-day-to-day-life-112a47a429d0).

7. **Search Engine Result Refining** – The manner in which users respond to a set of search results provide machine learning with data to build a predictive pattern to improve future search results. Google, Bing, etc., use such backend algorithms. 'Every time you execute a search, the algorithms at the backend keep a watch at how you respond to the results.' (https://medium.com/app-affairs/9-applications-of-machine-learning-from-day-to-day-life-112a47a429d0).

8. **Product Recommendations** – The users browsing patterns on shopping websites assists machine learning to predict and recommend the desired products. 'On the basis of your behaviour with the website/app, past purchases, items liked or added to cart, brand preferences etc., the product recommendations are made.' (https://medium.com/app-affairs/9-applications-of-machine-learning-from-day-to-day-life-112a47a429d0).

9. **Online Fraud Detection** – Funds transfer patterns are learnt by machine learning to determine genuine and potentially fraudulent online transactions. 'The company uses a set of tools that helps them to compare millions of transactions taking place and distinguish between legitimate or illegitimate transactions taking place between the buyers and sellers.' (https://medium.com/app-affairs/9-applications-of-machine-learning-from-day-to-day-life-112a47a429d0)

Conclusion

The paper was on a discussion on the meaning, significance and potential applications of the theoretical foundations of computer science with respect to Algorithms Design and Analysis, Complexity Theory, Turing Machines, Finite Automata, Cryptography, and Machine Learning. An algorithm is any well-defined computational procedure that takes some value or sets of values as input and produces some values or sets of values as output (Cormen, T.H., et al, 2009). According to Vitanyi, P.M.B. (2012, p.2), a Turing machine consists of a finite program, called the finite control, capable of manipulating a linear list of cells, called the tape, using one access pointer, called the head.Cellular automata is an array of finite state machines (inter-related). Cellular automata are used in the field of biology, the most common example being John Conway's Game of Life. A universal Turing machine U is a Turing machine that can imitate the behavior of any other Turing machine T (Vitanyi, P.M.B., 2012, p.5).

Automata (singular : automation) are a particularly simple, but useful, model of computation which were were initially proposed as a simple model for the behavior of neurons (Rao, D.C., 2016, p.16). A model of computation is a mathematical abstraction of computers which is used by computer scientists to perform a rigorous study of computation. An automaton with a finite number of states is called a Finite Automaton (FA) or Finite State Machine (FSM). The Church-Turing Thesis states that the Turing machine is equivalent in computational ability to any general mathematical device for computation, including digital computers.

The important themes in Theoretical Computer Science (TCS) are:

1. *Efficiency*
   The common measures arecomputation time, memory, parallelism, randomness, etc.

2. *Impossibility results*
   Intellectual ancestors, which deals with impossibility of perpetual motion, impossibility of trisecting an angle, incompleteness theorem, undecidability, etc.

3. *Approximation*
   Approximately optimal answers is about algorithms that work "most of the time", mathematical characterizations that are approximate (e.g., approximate max-flow min-cut theorem).

4. *Central role of randomness*
   Randomized algorithms and protocols, probabilistic encryption, random graph models, probabilistic models of the WWW, etc., are part of this set.

5. *Reductions*
   The focus is on NP-completeness and other intractability results (including complexity-based cryptography).

References

AURORA, S., and Barak, B., (2009). *Key Questions in Complex Theory.* [Online]. Available from: https://home.cyber.ee/¬ahtbu/complexity_o_slides.pdf. [Accessed: 29 April 2019].

BEAL, V., (2019). *Cryptography.*[Online] Available from: *https://www.webopedia.com/TERM/C/cryptography.html.* [Accessed: 27 April 2019].

BAJPAI, P., (2019). The *10 Most Important Cryptocurrencies Other Than Bitcoin.* [Online]. Available from: https://www.investopedia.com/tech/most-important-cryptocurrencies-other-than-bitcoin/. [Accessed: 29 April 2019].

CORNMEN, T.H, Leiserson, C.E, Rivest, A.L, Stein, C. (2009). 3rd ed. *Introduction to Algorithms.* Cambridge: MIT Press.

CUNNINGHAM, R., (2003). *Complexity Theory.* (Presented at the British Education Research Association Research Conference. September, 2013), Edinburgh University.

DAFFODIL Software, (2017). *9 Applications of Machine Learning from Day-to-Day Life.* [Online]. Available from: https://medium.com/app-affairs/9-applications-of-machine-learning-from-day-to-day-life-112a47a429d0. [Accessed: 30 April 2019]

EUKHOST, (2006). *Importance Of Cryptography in Digital World.* [Online]. Available from: https://www.eukhost.com/blog/webhosting/importance-of-cryptography-in-degital-world/. [Accessed: 28 April 2019]

GILLISPIE, T., (2014). The Relevance of Algorithms, MIT Press, 2014.

GOLDRIECH, O., (2000)., *A Brief Survey on Complexity Theory.* Weizmann Institute of Science.

HITACHI ID Systems. (2019). *Authentication.* [Online]. Available from https://hitachi-id.com/resource/iam-concepts/authentication.html. [Accessed: 30 April 2019].

KABANDA, G., (2013). "African context for technological futures for digital learning and the endogenous growth of a knowledge economy ", Basic Journal of Engineering Innovation (BRJENG), Volume 1(2), April 2013, pages 32-52 http://basicresearchjournals.org/engineering/PDF/Kabanda.pdf

KESSLER, G.C., (2019). *An Overview of Cryptography.* [Online]. Available from: https://www.garykessler.net/library/crypto.html [Accessed: 30 April 2019].

NATIONAL Academies Press. (2018). *Decrypting the Encryption Debate*: A Framework for

Decision   Makers.[Online]   Available   from: https://www.nap.edu/read/25010/chapter/4#20. [Accessed: 28 April 2019].

RAO, D.C., Sahu, K.K., and Das, P.K., (2016), Theory of Computation Lecture Notes, Department of Computer Science and Engineering & Information Technology, Veer Surendra Sai University of Technology, India, 2016.

RUELLE, D., (1991). Chance and Chaos, New Jersey: Princeton University Press, 1991.

SMITHERMAN, S., (2014). Chaos and Complexity Theories: Creating Holes and Wholes in Curriculum, The Chaos and Complexity Theories SIG at the AERA Annual Meeting, San Diego, CA, on Thursday, April 15, 2004.

STATISTICAL ANALYSIS SYSTEM, (2019). *Machine Learning, What it is and why it matters.* [Online]. Available from: https://www.sas.com/en_us/insights/analytics/machine-learning.html [Accessed: 30 April 2019].

VITANYI, P.M.B., (2012). Turing Machines and Understanding Computational, Centrum Wiskunde & Informatica, 2012, http://www.researchgate.net

WALTER, D., (2016), *Computational Complexity Theory.* The Stanford Encyclopedia of Philosophy.Winter, *2016 ed.* Edward. N. Zalta (editor). [Online]. Available from: https://plato.stanford.edu/archives//win2016/entries/computational-complexity/. [Accessed 03 May 2018].

YOUR KNOWLEDGE HAS VALUE

- We will publish your bachelor's and master's thesis, essays and papers

- Your own eBook and book - sold worldwide in all relevant shops

- Earn money with each sale

Upload your text at www.GRIN.com
and publish for free